The Battle of Colenso

15 December 1899

SB Bourquin and
Gilbert Torlage

RAVAN PRESS

The Battle Book Series

- The Battle of Talana
- The Battle of Elandslaagte
- The Battle of Colenso
- The Battle of Spioenkop
- The Battle of Vaalkrans
- The Battle of the Thukela Heights
- The Siege of Ladysmith

First published in 1999

Ravan Press
P O Box 145, Randburg 2125

ISBN: 0 86975 500 5

DTP and design by: Heather Brooksbank, Resolution

Cover Design: David Selfe, Dark Horse Design

Cartography: Toni Bodington & Olive Anderson
Cartographic Unit, University of Natal (Pietermaritzburg)

Photographs and sketches from: the KwaZulu-Natal Provincial
Museum Service Collection

Lithographic repro by: 3 White Dogs

Contents

Anglo-Boer War Sites

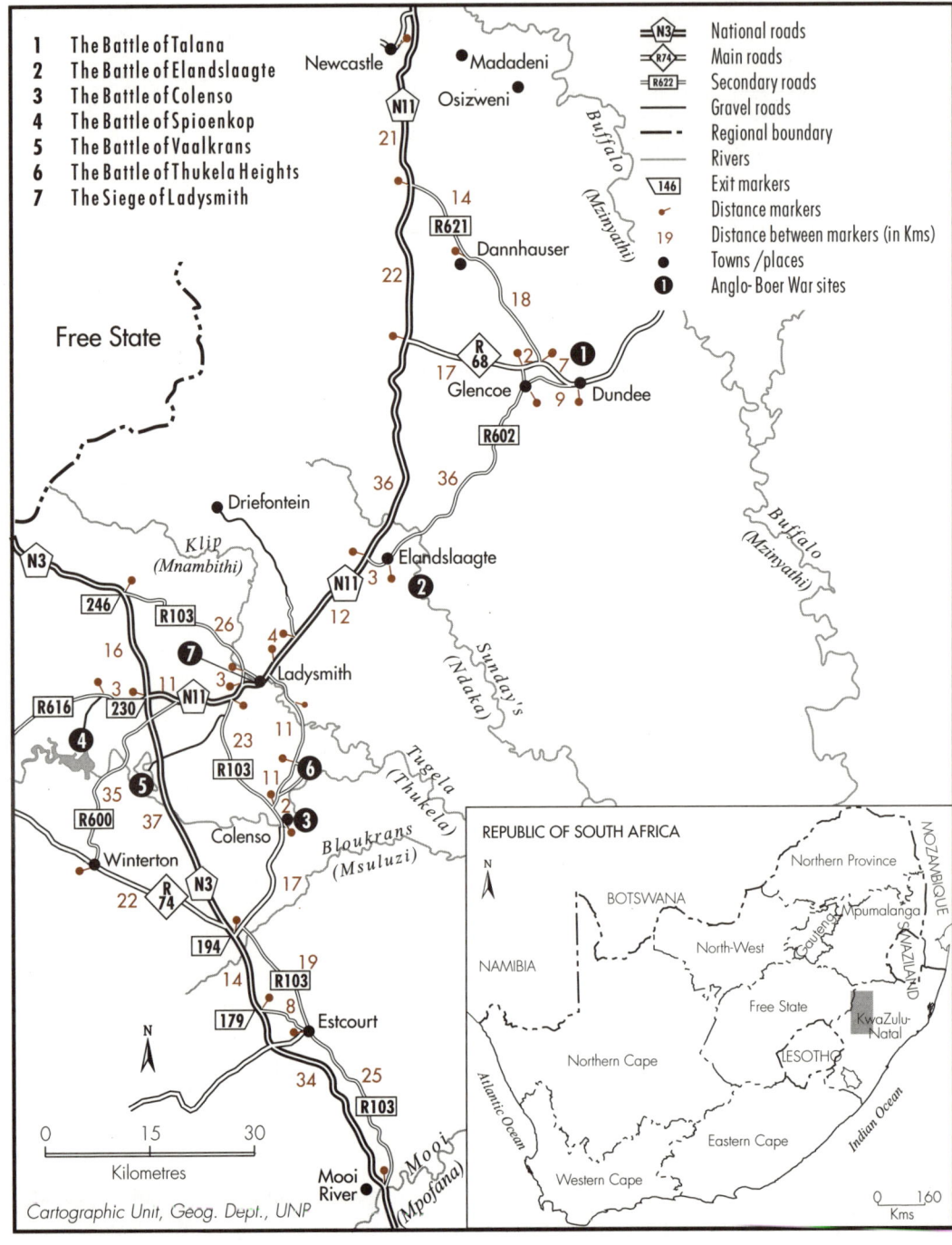

1 The Battle of Talana
2 The Battle of Elandslaagte
3 The Battle of Colenso
4 The Battle of Spioenkop
5 The Battle of Vaalkrans
6 The Battle of Thukela Heights
7 The Siege of Ladysmith

Legend:
- N3 — National roads
- R74 — Main roads
- R622 — Secondary roads
- Gravel roads
- Regional boundary
- Rivers
- 146 — Exit markers
- Distance markers
- 19 — Distance between markers (in Kms)
- Towns /places
- ❶ Anglo- Boer War sites

Free State

Newcastle
Madadeni
Osizweni
N11
21
14
R621
Dannhauser
22
18
R 68
17   2 7 ❶ Talana
Glencoe   9   Dundee
R602
36   36
Driefontein
Klip
(Mnambithi)
Elandslaagte
N11   3
❷
12
N3
246
R103   26
16   4
❼   3
230   11   N11   Ladysmith
R616   3   23   11
R103   11   ❻
❹   35   ❺   2   ❸
R600   37   Colenso
Winterton   Bloukrans
(Msuluzi)
22   R74   N3   17
194
14   R103   19
179   8
Estcourt
34   25
R103
Mooi
River   Mpofana
Buffalo
(Mzinyathi)
Sunday's
(Ndaka)
Tugela
(Thukela)

N

0   15   30
Kilometres

Cartographic Unit, Geog. Dept., UNP

REPUBLIC OF SOUTH AFRICA

N

BOTSWANA
Northern Province
MOZAMBIQUE
Gauteng   Mpumalanga
SWAZILAND
NAMIBIA
North-West
Free State
KwaZulu-Natal
Northern Cape
LESOTHO
Eastern Cape
Western Cape
Atlantic Ocean
Indian Ocean

0   160
Kms

Preface

This Battle Book series has been written to make information, photographs and maps of the most significant Anglo-Boer War sites in KwaZulu-Natal more readily available.

The books are not exhaustive studies of the various sites but rather field guides, designed to assist the reader in interpreting the terrain and understanding the events.

Although the Battle Books form a series, each book has been fully contextualised and can be followed on its own.

Contributors to this series share a long-term interest in the Anglo-Boer War and have each made their own unique contribution to the historiography and understanding of the conflict. With the assistance of an editorial committee, every effort has been made to maintain balance and accuracy.

A slightly flexible approach has been adopted to the spelling of names. As a general rule, the most recent spelling utilised on the state's Survey and Mapping 1:50 000 maps has been adopted. Thus for instance Laing's Nek becomes Lang's Nek. Where the name used to describe a topographical feature differs significantly from that in the historical literature to that appearing on the map, then the one used in the books and documents is adopted. The spelling of the river Thukela (Tugela) presents a slight problem. On the maps it is spelt as given in the brackets. However, in most current academic historical literature the former form has been adopted, which spelling has been followed in this series of books.

Introduction

The Anglo-Boer War was in its third week when the newly appointed Supreme Commander, South African Field Force, arrived on the Natal front. General Sir Redvers Buller, VC, was one of Britain's most famous soldiers and there were great expectations that he would bring the war in South Africa to a speedy end. Buller himself expressed the fear that the war might actually be over by the time he arrived in South Africa. He was no stranger to the African sub-continent, having been a subordinate commander of mounted men during the Anglo-Zulu War of 1879, where, as Lieutenant-Colonel, he earned a Victoria Cross at Hlobane. Now, although a general, he had not been associated with active troops for some 15 years, and doubted that he really was the right choice for the command of a whole army. This was the biggest British army ever to have been assembled in South Africa, and indeed the biggest army anywhere in the Empire, outside of Britain, since the Crimean War! Buller's own self-assessment, that he would be better as a second-in-command than in overall command, was, sad to say, not merely modest, but an accurate perception.

At the same time, it has been said that no British general had been so caring for the welfare of his soldiers as was Buller during his campaign. He made sure that they suffered as little hardship and discomfort as was militarily and humanly possible. For this concern, and also for his personal courage and coolness, he was idolised by his soldiers. That quality did not help him win battles, especially not against an enemy largely concealed on the battlefield, as at Colenso.

General Buller arrived at his headquarters at Frere and took over the command of the Natal Field Force from Lieutenant-General Sir Francis Clery on 6 December 1899, the day before his 60th birthday. The war had not gone well for Britain and certainly would not end speedily. Instead of the Boers being on the run, as expected, they were found dug in to fight and had inflicted heavy losses on the imperial armies facing them. They had besieged large British forces at Mafeking, Kimberley and Ladysmith. Worse was to follow, they impeded the march on Kimberley and beat off the British at Stormberg. The relief of Ladysmith now became Buller's primary objective.

At that stage Buller's army consisted, in round figures – both combat and service troops – of 15 900 infantry, 2 700 cavalry, 44 guns and 1 000 men in his Engineers, Army Medical and Army Service Corps.

S oon after the Boers had besieged Ladysmith, they decided to advance further south into Natal with a force of about 2 000 burghers led by Commandant-General Piet Joubert and General Louis Botha. It was their intention to damage the railway line in order to slow up the British column advancing from the coast to relieve Ladysmith. They left camp on 13 November 1899. On 14 November they fired on a British armoured train reconnoitering from Estcourt towards Colenso, and patrols advanced to near Estcourt where there was a British force of 2 300 awaiting reinforcements from the south.

On 15 November at 05:30 the armoured reconnaissance train left Estcourt again. On board were 164 officers and men of the Dublin Fusiliers and Durban Light Infantry, under the command of Captain Haldane. At Frere they met with some Natal police who informed them that the Boers were beyond Chieveley. Haldane therefore decided to press on. At Chieveley about 50 burghers and three wagons were spotted heading southwards and it was decided to return to Estcourt.

As the armoured train returned it was fired on and immediately picked up speed to get away. As it rounded a curve it crashed into a pile of stones laid on the track

Derailed trucks of the armoured train.

and some of the trucks were derailed. The Boers were ready and waiting. Under attack from both sides, the crew was rallied by Haldane, Captain Wylie of the Durban Light Infantry and the young newspaper correspondent, Winston Churchill.

The derailed trucks were detached and moved aside and the wounded piled on to the engine and tender. The remaining debris was pushed aside and a successful dash made to Estcourt. A relief column met the survivors at Ennersdale. Several casualties and prisoners were left behind. Churchill was one of the prisoners, captured as he tried to run away towards Frere station.

The Boers destroyed this rail bridge on 30 November 1899. On the right is a replacement trestle bridge completed by the British in April 1900.

Louis Botha (seated centre) and other Boer leaders near Colenso, a few days before the battle on 15 December 1899.

This success encouraged the Boers to advance further. They bypassed Estcourt on either side and met at Highlands, where they cut the rail and telegraph lines. The British force at Estcourt was now isolated from the next one at Mooi River. The Boers launched a half-hearted attack on Mooi River. Between 17 and 21 November the British commander at Estcourt, Major-General Hildyard, despatched several ineffective expeditions to try to dislodge the Boers from the Willow Grange area.

Hildyard then decided to launch a night attack on the Boer positions on Brynbella Hill – about halfway between Estcourt and Mooi River. The force advanced from Estcourt on the afternoon of 22 November in intense heat and that night occurred the most devastating thunderstorm in local memory. Several men on both sides were struck by lightning. Artillery, including a naval gun laboriously dragged up Beacon Hill, could not be used for most of the subsequent battle.

In the early hours of 23 November, two regiments, the East Surreys and West Yorks, marching from Beacon Hill to Brynbella Hill, on either side of a stone wall, mistook each other for the Boers. In the ensuing chaos eight men were killed. The British regrouped and continued with their advance and by dawn on the 23rd the Boers had been driven off Brynbella Hill at little cost to the attackers, despite the incident at the stone wall. However, the arrival of Boer reinforcements and artillery support enabled the burghers to easily drive off the British force, inflicting approximately 78 casualties against four of their own.

Despite the minor victory at Willow Grange, the Boers decided not to press home their advantage and endeavour to capture Estcourt. The Boers, realising that they were in an increasingly precarious position between the British forces in Mooi River and Estcourt, decided to retire to the Thukela (Tugela) River at Colenso.

They went via Weenen to hide their final intentions. The expedition had served no purpose. The British had also missed an opportunity to attack them during this retirement.

Boer defensive position at the Thukela

The Boer force facing Buller had dug in on the hills north of the Thukela River and Colenso, and were determined to make the most of the elevated position to prevent the British from crossing and relieving Ladysmith. They were commanded by Louis Botha, who at age 37, was the youngest Boer general. His youth and lack of experience were more than compensated for by his exceptional leadership qualities, his energy and fine grasp of strategy.

At a council of war on 30 November the Boer leaders discussed the siting of their main defence line. Botha made an audacious proposal. His plan was to move forward from the safety of the high ground, down towards the river, where he hoped to take the attacking British in the open by surprise. His plan was approved. To ensure secrecy all trenches and breastworks near the river were constructed at night and covered with grass and bushes. Soil dug from trenches was scattered in the grass.

Boer trenches from which they repulsed Major-General Hart's men at "the loop".

To distract and mislead the British, Botha had other trenches dug, on the high ground where they would be expected and could be seen by the British. In addition, dummy gun barrels made from flattened and rolled up corrugated iron were mounted in mock gun emplacements. In the event of an attack the burghers were under instructions to hold their fire until a pre-arranged signal was given – a shot from a howitzer which was placed in the Colenso Koppies (koppie – low hill). Botha hoped that Buller's men would march as far into the trap as possible to ensure maximum casualties.

The Boer force was deployed in four main positions, each group having a specific task. In trenches north of a big loop in the Thukela River were placed the Ermelo and Soutpansberg commandos and the Swaziland Police to guard the drifts there. A little further upstream, behind a spur of the high ground were Free State burghers and members of the Middelburg and Johannesburg commandos, commanded by General Fourie. In the event of a British attack being repulsed from the loop area, Fourie was to cross the Thukela River and cut off the British retreat. The hills immediately west and north of Colenso were occupied by the Johannesburg Police, Heidelberg and Krugersdorp commandos and a few Vryheid burghers. They were placed there because Botha anticipated that the British would use the road bridge. The final group, the Boksburg and the Soutpansberg commandos, occupied the Hlangwane Hill, which was on the south (British) side of the river, which turned north between it and Colenso. They were in line with the other Boer units and were posted there to prevent the British artillery enfilading the Boer positions to the west.

By mid-December Botha's forces consisted of approximately 4 500 men, supported by five pieces of artillery. The artillery was placed with utmost care and carefully concealed. Overlooking the loop in the Thukela were two 75mm Creusot field guns and in the hills overlooking Colenso were a 75mm Krupp field gun, a 37mm Maxim-Nordenfeldt (called a Pom-Pom by the British) and a 120mm Howitzer.

At Colenso the iron railway bridge, 154 meters long, was demolished by the Boers with five explosive charges, but the iron road bridge was left intact. The Thukela River was wide and deep above and below the bridge and fordable only at a limited number of places. Most of these fords had been dug up by the Boers to make them difficult to cross.

Buller's initiative

In order to defeat his opponents and relieve Ladysmith, Buller, with the force at his disposal could do one of three things: (1) assault the centre of the Boer position at Colenso; (2) turn the Boer right flank to the west on the upper Thukela; (3) turn the left flank east of Colenso. All three involved crossing the river in the face of an active enemy. Buller found it difficult to choose a course of action.

General Sir Redvers Buller, VC, commander of the British force at Colenso. He was a vastly experienced officer. Several years in the War Office and age (60 years) undermined his fitness.

The maps he had at his disposal had been hastily prepared from farm surveys and were inadequate and incorrect; so were some military sketches of the terrain made by some officers. (One sketch "made on the spot by a military draughtsman" actually shows Colenso and Hlangwane on the wrong side, that is the north bank of the Thukela.)

On 8 December from Frere Buller telegraphed Lord Lansdowne, Secretary of State for War, in London: "I find I cannot force the Boer defences between here and Ladysmith and must turn them. To do this I have to march 50 miles." So, there he was, thinking hard about a move west, in full view of the Boers, parallel with the Thukela River; and there he was staring at his farm maps and focusing on Potgieter's Drift (which was upstream in the Spioenkop area) and the heights beyond. On 11 December he issued orders for the army to march to the upper Thukela. Early on 12 December Buller ordered a brigade and eight naval guns onto a low rise (now Naval Gun Hill) about six kilometres south of Colenso to cover the planned march. Botha incorrectly interpreted this movement as the long anticipated advance on Colenso.

Suddenly, in the evening of the same day Buller changed his mind and called a halt. He decided to make a frontal attack against the Boer position. In England as well as Ladysmith a decisive stroke was anxiously anticipated. Perhaps the news of British defeats at Stormberg on 11 December and at Magersfontein on 12 December upset Buller's judgement. He had reiterated to his staff, the War Office in London, and to Lieutenant-Major General Sir George White commander in Ladysmith, that a frontal attack would be "too costly" and now, he was going to make it.

On 13 December Buller signalled to White that he would be coming through Colenso. On that same morning Buller's artillery opened fire on the Boer positions at 07:15 and continued for three hours. As instructed the Boers did not fire a single round in response. On 14 December the naval battery moved 2 700 metres closer and fired all morning and afternoon on the Boer positions. Again there was no response. Most of the British shells burst well beyond the Boer positions or on their dummy ones. It became evident to the Boers that

HT)BIRDS EYE VIEW OF FRERE CAMP-THE LARGEST BRITISH FORCE ASSEMBLED UNDER CANVASS FOR A CAMPAIGN-UPWARDS OF 25000 NAVAL

British camp at Frere.

the British had no idea where their real positions were. At the same time Buller's force advanced from Frere to beyond Chieveley. Where were the Boers? The British van was well within range of the guns. Only individuals and small groups of three or four, could occasionally be seen moving about. Botha's strict discipline kept his men in their trenches. Not a single Boer gun gave away its location by a premature shot.

The British bombardment and advance of their army did create a crisis. On 13 December, after sunset, the entire Soutpansberg commando and several Boksburgers, feeling threatened retired from Hlangwane. At a council of war several Boer commandants suggested that the burghers in the forward positions return to the high ground further back from the river and much against Botha's will, vacate Hlangwane entirely. Hlangwane remained unoccupied for 24 hours, unnoticed by the British. Botha's plan to surprise Buller's force was in the balance. Another council of war was held the following morning. Botha, armed with telegrams from President Paul Kruger urging re-occupation of Hlangwane, managed to persuade the Boer commandos to re-occupy the hill. The force was determined by lot and fell to the Wakkerstroom and Standerton commandos, and wards of the Middelburg, Soutpansberg and Ermelo commandos, a force comprising eight hundred to a thousand men. The commandants also agreed to hold the forward positions.

Buller's plan of attack

Late on 14 December Buller was ready for the next phase of his attack: the frontal assault on the Boer position. The British had little idea of where the main Boer positions were. Buller's maps were deficient and reconnaissance had been inadequate.

Late on the 14th Buller issued his officers with orders for a general attack on the following day, 15 December. The plan was for a frontal three-pronged attack by three infantry brigades on the Boer trenches, the very thing he had declared impracticable a few days before. The remaining two infantry brigades were to be held in reserve, covering the gaps between the centre and the wings, so as to be able to reinforce rapidly either of the two main points of attack or the far right wing if it should get into difficulty.

An army of 15 000 soldiers and 44 guns were poised to challenge 4 500 entrenched or concealed burghers and their five guns. The left prong, the 5th (Irish) Brigade, commanded by Major-General Hart, was to cross the Thukela River via Bridle Drift, shown on the British map to be immediately west of the confluence of the Thukela and Doring Spruit.

Colonel Long, commander of the artillery at Colenso.

The maps showed the confluence to be immediately upstream of the loop, whereas in reality it was just downstream of the loop. Poor reconnaissance had failed to reveal this mapping error. Once across, the brigade was to occupy the Colenso Koppies. The centre prong, the 2nd Brigade, commanded by Major-General Hildyard, was to cross via the iron bridge and join the 5th Brigade in the koppies. The right prong, the mounted brigade under Colonel Lord Dundonald, accompanied by one battery of field artillery, was to take

Hlangwane and from it enfilade any Boer positions in the koppies. The mounted brigade was also to protect Hildyard's right flank. The 4th and 6th Brigades were in reserve.

The artillery was divided up into two main groupings. The 1st Brigade Division Royal Field Artillery, commanded by Lieutenant-Colonel Hunt, was made up of twelve 15 pounders, and six naval guns were under Lieutenant Ogilvy, RN. However, Colonel Long, who commanded all the artillery, was ordered by Buller to personally take command of all these 18 guns and proceed to a point from which they were to "prepare the crossing for" Hildyard's men. On the left the 2nd Brigade Division Royal Field Artillery, commanded by Lieutenant-Colonel Parsons, comprising twelve 15 pounder guns, was to follow the 4th Brigade, and to take up a position from which it could enfilade the Colenso Koppies and support Hart's attack if required.

The orders were all relatively straightforward, but issued too late for any of the commanders to reconnoitre beforehand or to discuss and clear up any ambiguities. None of Buller's officers questioned these orders. The brigades began their advance shortly before dawn on Friday 15 December.

The attack begins

That night Botha slept on the sandbags used to build the howitzer emplacement in the Koppies. At approximately 01:00 on 15 December some Boers noticed several small lights in the direction of the British camp. They soon realised that the long-awaited British attack was going to take place that morning. Word was passed along the trenches, to warn the other burghers.

In semi-darkness, early on 15 December, the British men and guns silently left their camps and proceeded across grassy flat land towards the Thukela. As the sky began to lighten the Boers noticed the "long, broad, brown line" of men advancing towards them. At 05:20 the six naval guns on Naval Gun Hill opened fire. The Boers did not reply.

The trap on the left

Hart's brigade, the left prong, consisting of approximately 3 500 men, gathered in complete darkness and absolute silence. They paraded at 04:00 and after twenty minutes marched off and advanced steadily through the cool morning air. The silence was broken only by their steady tramp and crunching of the fresh grass. Hart had with him the erroneous map, an African guide and a colonist interpreter to assist him in finding his way to the Bridle Drift. The African guide apparently believed he was to lead them to the drift at the head of the loop – quite literally into a death trap. Hart's force initially advanced to the north-west and then north. Hart was preceded by cavalry scouts who warned him on three occasions that the Boers were in strength to his front and left. He replied that he would ignore the men on his left as he was going straight ahead. As he approached the western base in the loop, he sensed that he was in the wrong place and the map had misled him. He enquired further of the African guide, who pointed into the loop and stated that was where the drift lay.

Hart's men, massed closely together, turned into the loop. Just after 06:00 a Boer gun on the heights to the north opened fire. Its first shell passed harmlessly over the British force, the second landed between two battalions, and the third brought nine men to the ground.

The Boer riflemen opened fire. The British began deploying. It was difficult for them to determine where the fire was coming from. Casualties mounted. Apart from one or two small depressions and an occasional anthill there was no cover. Hart's men tried valiantly to return the fire – but they could not see the well-concealed Boers. The companies became hopelessly intermingled and confused – casualties continued to mount as the Boers poured on a steady fire and pinned them down.

BATTLE FIELD
OF Colenso
15 Decbr 1899

A Boer 75mm Creusot gun overlooking "the loop", visible on the right. Hart's men marching in close formation into "the loop", completely exposed, must have made an almost unbelievable sight to the gunners.

The scene was described in the history of the Royal Dublin Fusiliers:

" There was one ceaseless rattle of Mausers, and a constant hum of bullets only drowned by the scream of shells... There was no control, no cohesion, no arrangement in the attack... Nobody knew where the drift was, nobody had a clear idea of what was happening. All pushed forward blindly, animated by the sole idea of reaching the river bank."

Parsons, with his 12 guns, tried to support Hart's men, but because the Boers were so well concealed the British guns achieved nothing.

Major-General Fitzroy Hart, commander of the ill-fated 5th (Irish) Brigade.

B uller, watching through his telescope, was horrified at the spectacle: "Hart has got himself into a devil of a mess down there – get him out!" Thus he ordered Major-General Lyttelton of the 4th Brigade to assist in extricating the Irish from the loop.

Buller (on left) and other officers viewing the battle.

Lyttelton moved with the Rifle Brigade and the Durham Light Infantry to the mouth of the loop where he tried to provide covering fire. The Irish were initially reluctant to obey the unwelcome order but eventually came stumbling back from the loop, leaving over 500 men dead, wounded and captured. By 08:00, just two hours after the first shots, Hart's brigade was in retreat. The Boers missed the opportunity to cut it off. Fourie's force just upstream never moved, despite being ordered to do so three times.

The Irish Brigade under fire at "the loop". It would appear that a few men managed to cross the river but were captured.

Botha, on the Colenso Koppies, watched in helpless rage as the opportunity slipped away. Subsequently he commented that Fourie and his men had "continued to watch the battle, sitting manfully on the mountain".

The Battle of Colenso

On the fifteenth of December, in eighteen ninety nine,
We tried to drive the Boers from their strong Colenso line,
Before us flowed a river deep - Tugela was its name,
And the general commanding was Buller of great fame.
The Irish brigade was on the left, and under Hart's command,
Four splendid regiments were there, who made a desperate stand,
But it was unavailing, for the Boers were far too strong,
And many a gallant hero fell, as we boldly marched along.

Chorus
Then here's to the gallant Dublins, and the brave old Connaughts too,
The Border lads undaunted, and the Inniskillings true,
Side by side, they fought and died, each man beside his "pal",
Fighting for England's honour on the border of Natal.

Towards Tugela's banks at dawn, we slowly made our way.
The hills looked grim and silent as the burghers stood at bay;
Some thought of Home, of those they loved, and friends whom they held dear,
Whilst others thought of Him, above, and prayed, though not through fear.
But when from out the roseate east the sun in splendour rose,
It shone on British soldiers who did not fear their foes,
Upholding England's name and fame, and fighting for their Queen
It was the grandest sight, my lads, that I had ever seen.

Suddenly an awful roar was heard upon our right,
The Naval guns had opened fire, and so began the fight,
The foe replied: soon shot and shell were flying all around,
And many a gallant British lad lay groaning on the ground.
The brave old Dubs pressed forward with a slow and steady pace,
The Connaughts close behind them, stern resolve on every face,
The Border lads were close at hand, the Inniskillings too,
And then, those regiments showed the Boers what British pluck
can do.

For hours, around these gallant lads the shot like hailstones fell,
And many a bullet found its mark in that infernal hell;
With sad downcast face we heard the order to retire,
The position was too strong to take beneath that falling fire.
Sadly from off the battlefield we slowly made our way,
Grieving for fallen comrades that were killed on that sad day;
That night the moon with silvery rays shone down upon the
ground,
Where many a brave Irish soldier lad, his last lane home had
found.

Composed by One of the Dubs, Spearman's Camp
1 February 1900

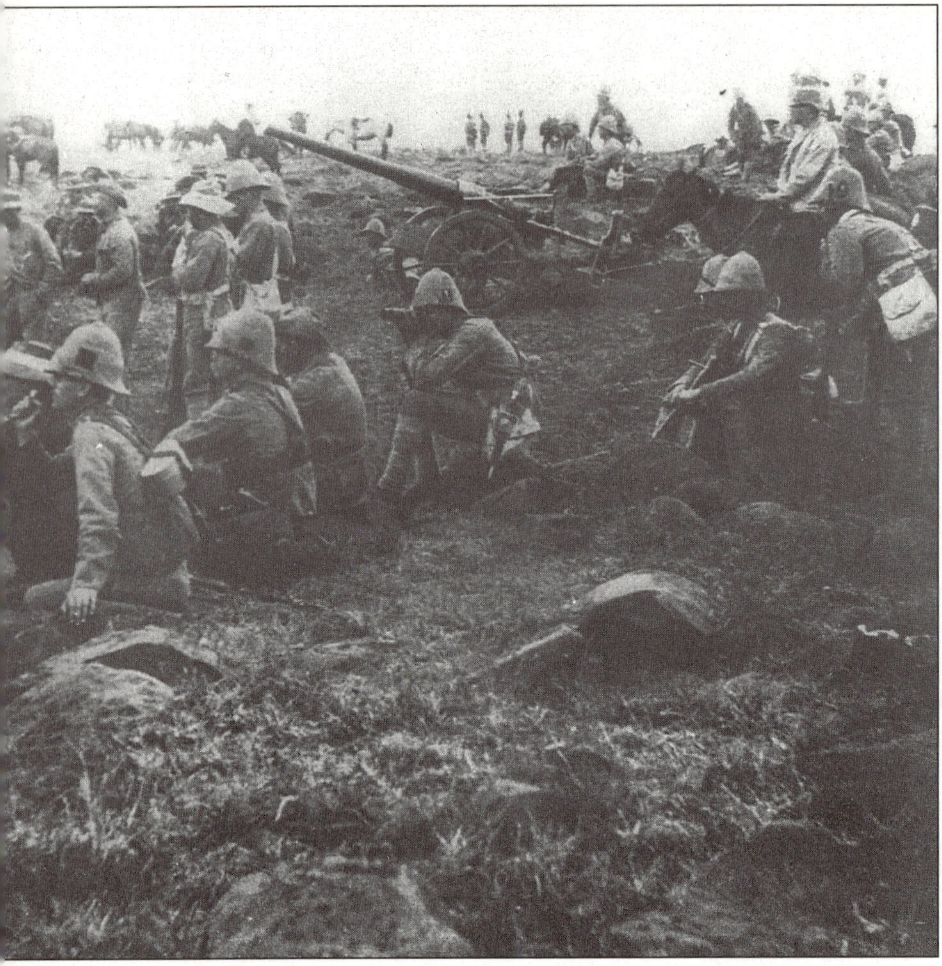

British troops beside a 12 pounder naval gun during the battle of Colenso.

Stalemate on the right

Meanwhile, on the right, Dundonald's column of 800 men proceeded rapidly towards the dense bush on Hlangwane. It was soon obvious that the Boers occupied the hill. That and the steep and broken nature of the slopes, would preclude deploying artillery on the summit.

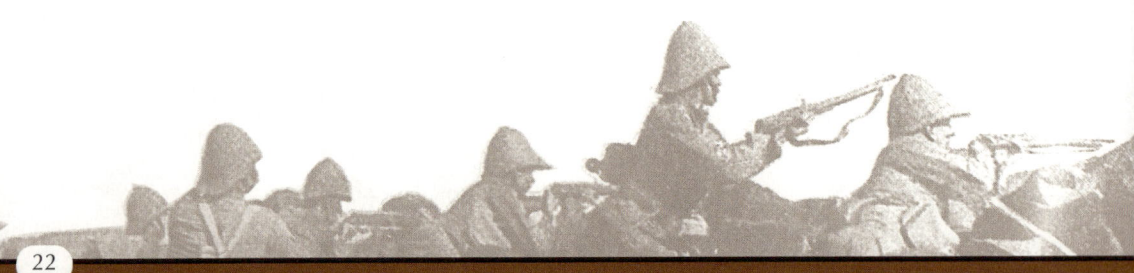

General Louis Botha aged 37 and commander of the Boer forces at Colenso. He was the youngest general in the Boer forces. His tactical foresight, energy and strong leadership assisted in repulsing the British forces.

Dundonald therefore brought his artillery into action short of Hlangwane, firing on the hill and the Colenso Koppies. Upon reaching the broken and bushy area of the Gomba stream at 07:15, the cavalry dismounted and advanced on foot. As they came within range the Boers opened fire from their concealed positions behind rocks and bushes, and checked the advance.

Dundonald believed, as did Botha, that Hlangwane was the key to the successful occupation of the Colenso Koppies. He requested reinforcements from Barton, so that he could penetrate between the hill and the Thukela, threatening the burghers' retreat route and precipitating their withdrawal. Barton refused to assist, possibly prompted by the problems elsewhere. Dundonald could make no progress, and the battle below Hlangwane developed into a stalemate.

Artillery exposed at the centre

Hildyard's 2nd Brigade, the central prong of the attack, set off from camp a short time before the Irish Brigade, towards the railway line and then headed northwards along it. Barton's Brigade (6th Brigade) and Long's artillery, slightly east of Hildyard's men, were advancing northwards at the same time. Long had instructions to prepare the way for Hildyard's men and therefore moved ahead of the infantry. Soon the horse-drawn and lighter 15-pounder guns of the 14th and 66th Batteries drew ahead of the six heavier, ox-drawn naval guns.

Before Long departed from camp Buller indicated to him on a "rough map in general terms" where he was to come into action and what his objective was to be. As Long approached the area where he believed he should come into action, he searched for a suitable site from which to fire. Soon after 06:00 heavy firing was heard to his left – the start of the battle in the loop. Anxious to lend support, he ordered the 12 field guns – 14th and 66th Batteries Royal Field Artillery – forward to a position about 80 metres beyond a broad, shallow gully, which ran from east to west. The site was open and flat. By this time the artillery's patrols had returned from the river and reported no Boers south of it. The danger immediately across the river remained undetected.

The burghers concealed to the north-west, north and north-east of Colenso viewed with deep anxiety the preparations to fire the guns. On Botha's orders they held their fire. He hoped that the mass of Hildyard's infantry, still some distance off, would come close enough to be fired on or, better still, cross the iron bridge.

Eventually the burghers' nerve began to fail, and they urged Botha to give the signal to fire; the British guns were a mere 1 000 metres away from where they lay hidden. Soon after 06:00 the burghers, supported by three guns in the koppies, opened fire on Long's men – probably on Botha's orders, but this cannot be stated with absolute certainty.

The 69th Battery drawn up in line at Ladysmith. The batteries would have formed up in the same way on the morning of 15 December 1899. The Battery Commander sits on his horse in front. The three section commanders are in front with their gun sections. The sergeant or No 1 of each gun is alongside his lead driver. Behind each gun is its associated ammunition wagon. In the rear of the battery is the quartermaster sergeant and his staff.

Because of the great distance the Boers' fire was not effective initially. Preparation of the field guns continued and they came into action. Approximately 400 metres back at a large gully, the naval guns also came into action despite most of the drivers having run away as soon as the firing began. The British opened fire, but the Boers were well posted and concealed and were using smokeless powder, making it extremely difficult to locate them. Therefore the British shell fire was not that effective.

As soon as the Boers opened fire all the black drivers with the naval guns, except the front two, fled. The front drivers merely turned up their collars and continued with their duties. This illustration is therefore incorrect.

After a short while the Boers got the range of the British guns and British casualties mounted rapidly. Long himself was wounded and taken to the shelter of the shallow gully a little further back. After a while the British guns' first supply of ammunition was expended, and the second supply was brought forward.

A request for additional ammunition from approximately five kilometres back was delayed by the death of Captain AH Goldie and the wounding of Captain FA Elton, in the wagon line. Despite the terrific fire inflicting heavy casualties on them, the gun crews at the field batteries continued to serve their guns with admirable courage and discipline. Members of the Krugersdorp Commando stated subsequently that the artillery fire had made it difficult for them to maintain a proper fire on the gunners. Ammunition ran out and at 07:15 Long called his men back to the cover of the gully.

Long has been criticised for recklessness in taking his guns too far forward. At no stage was he shown precisely where to come into action. He believed that he was trying to fulfil his order to advance to a point "from which (to) prepare the crossing for the 2nd (Hildyard's) Brigade". He admitted in a later report that he did "get closer than I intended", but explained that in the early morning light distances were deceptive. By coming into action so close to the Boers he did force them to open fire early and reveal their position. Hildyard's men, warned by the unexpected and heavy firing of the dangers that lay before them, were ordered to halt several hundred metres further back.

Hart's brigade was in disarray and Long's guns were quite useless and abandoned. Buller, at Naval Gun Hill, was informed of Long's predicament. After a while he decided to ride across personally and see for himself. On his way he met Hildyard and informed him that the original attack was to be given up, but he was to advance two battalions to help extricate the guns. In fact Hildyard had already sent forward two battalions, the Queens and Devons. The Queens were making their way into the fire zone in the tiny village of Colenso and the Devons were on their way across the veld to the guns. At about 09:30 two companies arrived at the gully where Long lay.

Loss of the guns

Buller rode on to where the naval guns were at the large gully and came under fire. Captain Hughes of the Royal Army Medical Corps was killed alongside him, and he himself was hit on the chest by spent shell fragments. He ordered the naval guns in the gully to be withdrawn and the additional ammunition, being taken to Long's guns, be taken back to camp. He seemed to believe that it would be too dangerous to bring Long's field guns back into action. He told his ADC, Captain Schofield, to try to retrieve the guns. Volunteers were called for from men sheltering in the large gully. They would have to dash over a few hundred metres of flat, open veld, exposed to heavy fire, in order to reach the guns. Despite the danger, teams of men and horses dashed forward, hitched up two guns and dragged them to safety.

Captain Walter Congreve, one of the volunteers who tried to rescue the guns, described his ride as follows,

"My first bullet went through my left sleeve and just made the point of my elbow bleed. Next a clod of earth caught me no end of a smack on the other arm, then my horse got one and then my right leg, my horse another, and that settled the question. He plunged and I fell off about a hundred yards from the guns we were going to."

Another three attempts to save the remaining guns were made, but failed with heavy casualties. Buller decided to abandon the guns.

Shortly before 11:00 he ordered Hildyard's brigade to retire to camp. At Colenso, Hildyard's men also experienced difficulty withdrawing from their forward positions. Meanwhile Buller rode across to Dundonald and instructed him to retire as well. It took Dundonald a number of hours to extricate his men and under constant harassment return to camp.

"At No 5 Gun, 14th Battery, two men were left unwounded – one laid the gun, while the other ran backwards and forwards with the ammunition. In a few moments these two men were shot down, and the gun left alone."

By 14:30 the withdrawal was well under way along the entire front. Some of the stragglers only arrived back in camp after 17:00.

Buller's decision to abandon the ten guns was a curious one. He still had over 30 guns and large numbers of men which he could have deployed to make it very costly if not impossible for the Boers to cross over the Thukela and take them. Then under cover of darkness he could have retrieved them.

Indian stretcher bearers. At the beginning of the war approximately 1 000 Natal Indians offered their services as unpaid ambulance assistants. They were of great help to the wounded at Colenso. This photograph was possibly taken at Rietfontein.

Perhaps the blow on his chest had affected his judgement. Furthermore, he disliked seeing men suffer, and the soldiers would have had to go without water for 18 hours. "No water, not a breath of air, and not a particle of shade and a sun which I have never felt hotter even in India," was one soldier's description of conditions.

The Boers decided to capture the abandoned guns. They crossed the Thukela at about 17:00 and advanced towards the prize. They were met by unexpected rifle fire from two sections of the Devonshire Regiment who had occupied a crack in the ground in front of the guns and had not realised that a retreat had been ordered. They offered a spirited resistance until eventually forced to surrender as the Boers arrived in ever greater numbers. The guns were taken and sent to Pretoria and ultimately distributed to various fronts to be used against the British. (Some accounts suggest that a good deal of ammunition was also captured, but Long's report makes it clear that the gunners left their guns only when all the ammunition had been expended. Recent research has confirmed this.)

The British guns and ammunition wagons captured by the Boers at Colenso, en route to Pretoria, on arrival at Newcastle Station.

Louis Botha reading messages of congratulation to his men.

Conclusion

In addition to the ten guns lost, British casualties were approximately 143 men killed, 756 wounded and 240 captured and missing, according to the Official History. The Boer loss was negligible by comparison, being eight killed and 30 wounded.

The first attempt to relieve Ladysmith had failed. Poor British reconnaissance was the major reason. It failed to discover the Boer positions. This is not to detract from Botha's preparations and tactics, based on an intimate knowledge of the terrain and correctly anticipating the British attacks.

On 16 December the Boers celebrated the "Day of the Vow" with a religious service. It was an impressive occasion. There was much to be grateful for. Afterwards Generals Schalk Burger and Botha addressed the men, speaking from on top of one of the captured guns. Messages of congratulation streamed into Botha's headquarters from both republics, including ones from Presidents Kruger and Steyn.

In a message to Kruger the evening after the battle, Botha described the day's events as follows:

"The Lord of our fathers has today given us a brilliant victory. We have repulsed the enemy on all sides, at three different points. We allowed them, under violent bombardment from their side, to advance 12 guns up to a point very near the river. As soon as these were unlimbered, we opened fire with our Mausers, killing the gunners and disorganising them to such an extent that they only succeeded in recovering two of their guns. We took the other ten – big beautiful cannons – together with 13 [actually 12] full ammunition wagons. (Evidence suggests that these wagons were in fact empty.) About 150 of their best men, those who stormed so bravely time after time, were taken prisoner. Among them are several officers. The enemy's losses must have been terrible. They are lying one on another – I think possibly 2 000 men. We have about 30 killed and wounded. I shall later send you exact reports. With a thankful heart I can congratulate you and the Afrikaner people on this brilliant victory... Guns already brought through the river, and I respectfully request the Government to proclaim a general day of prayer to thank Him who gave us this victory."

This request was granted.

Lieutenant Freddy Roberts (son of Field Marshal Roberts) on the right, riding forward in an effort to save the guns. Roberts fell mortally wounded and was dragged into cover. He, along with six others were awarded Victoria Crosses for their gallantry during the battle.

Buller tried to blame Long for his reverse. "I was sold by a damned gunner," he complained. In reality, however, Long probably saved Hildyard's column from the same fate that befell Hart's force – and he could certainly not be held responsible for Hart's difficulties on the left. Buller was shaken by this reverse and became quite pessimistic.

In a telegraph to the Secretary of State for War he reported:

> "My failure today raises a serious question. I don't think I am now strong enough to relieve White... I do not think either a gun or a Boer was seen by us all day... My view is that I ought to let Ladysmith go, and occupy good positions for the defence of South Natal, and let time help us..."

The War Office and British Cabinet responded swiftly to this crisis by appointing Field-Marshal Lord FS Roberts as the new Commander-in-Chief in South Africa and General Lord HH Kitchener as his Chief of Staff, and relegated Buller to command in the Natal front, which would require his full attention. Buller accepted his demotion with good grace and, for a while, went on the defensive with his forces. He still had far more men and guns at his disposal than his adversaries had. It was merely a matter of time before he made the next move to relieve Ladysmith.

Opposing forces

Boer

Commanding Officer: General Louis Botha

Western wing: Free Staters, Middelburg and Johannesburg commandos

Loop sector: Ermelo, Boksburg and Soutpansberg commandos, Swaziland Police and two 75mm Creusot guns

Colenso Koppies: Heidelberg, Krugersdorp, Soutpansberg and Vryheid (portion only) commandos, Johannesburg Police, one 120mm Krupp howitzer, one 75mm Krupp and one Maxim-Nordenfeldt

Hlangwane: Wakkerstroom and Standerton commandos and elements of the Middelburg, Soutpansberg and Ermelo commandos

Commanding officer: General Sir Redvers Buller VC

Artillery: Naval Brigade and 14 guns; Royal Field Artillery – 7th, 14th, 64th, 66th and 73rd batteries

Infantry:

2nd Brigade: Major-General Hildyard's – 2nd Royal West Surrey Regiment (Queens), 2nd Devonshire Regiment, 2nd East Surrey Regiment, 2nd West Yorkshire Regiment

4th Brigade: Major-General Lyttelton's – 2nd Scottish Rifles, 3rd King's Royal Rifle Corps, 1st Rifle Brigade, 1st Durham Light Infantry

5th Brigade: Major-General Hart's – 2nd Royal Dublin Fusiliers, 1st Connaught Rangers, 1st Border Regiment, 1st Royal Inniskilling Fusiliers

6th Brigade: Major-General Barton's – 1st Royal Welsh Fusiliers, 2nd Royal Irish Fusiliers, 2nd Royal Scots Fusiliers, 2nd Royal Fusiliers

Mounted Brigade: Colonel Lord Dundonald – 1st Royal Dragoons, 13th Hussars, Bethune's Mounted Infantry, Thorneycroft's Mounted Infantry, South African Light Horse, Composite Regiment

---

Orders by Lieut.-General Sir Francis Clery, K.C.B., Commanding South Natal Field Force.

Chieveley
14th December, 1899. 10 p.m.

1. The enemy is entrenched in the kopjes north of Colenso bridge. One large camp is reported to be near Ladysmith road, about five miles north-west of Colenso. Another large camp is reported in the hills which lie north of the Tugela in a northerly direction from Hlangwhane Hill .

2. It is the intention of the General Officer Commanding to force the passage of the Tugela tomorrow.

3. The 5th brigade will move from its present camping ground at 4.30 a.m., and march towards Bridle Drift, immediately west of the junction of Doornkop Spruit (Doring Spruit) and the Tugela. The brigade will cross at this point, and after crossing move along the left bank of the river towards the kopjes north of the iron bridge.

4. The 2nd brigade will move from its present camping ground at 4 a.m., and passing south of the present camping ground of No. 1 and No. 2 Divisional troops, will march in the direction of the iron bridge at Colenso. The brigade will cross at this point and gain possession of the kopjes north of the iron bridge.

5. The 4th brigade will advance at 4.30 a.m., to a point between Bridle Drift and the railway, so that it can support either the 5th or the 2nd brigade.

6. The 6th brigade (less a half-battalion to escort the baggage) will move at 4 a.m., east of the railway in the direction of Hlangwhane Hill to a position where it can protect the right flank of the 2nd brigade, and, if necessary, support it or the mounted troops referred to later as moving towards Hlangwhane Hill.

7. The Officer Commanding mounted brigade will move at 4 a.m., with a force of 1 000 men and one battery of No. 1 brigade division in the direction of Hlangwhane Hill; he will cover the right flank of the general movement, and will endeavour to take up a position on Hlangwhane Hill, whence he will enfilade the kopjes north of the iron bridge.The Officer Commanding mounted troops will also detail two forces of 300 and 500 men to cover the right and left flanks respectively and protect the baggage.

8. The 2nd brigade division, Royal Field artillery, will move at 4.30 a.m., following the 4th brigade, and will take up a position whence it can enfilade the kopjes north of the iron bridge. This brigade division will act on any orders it receives from Major-General Hart.

   The six naval guns (two 4.7-in. and four 12-pr.) now in position north of the 4th brigade, will advance on the right of the 2nd brigade division, Royal Field artillery.

   No.1 brigade division, Royal Field artillery (less one battery detached with mounted brigade), will move at 3.30 a.m., east of the railway and proceed under cover of the 6th brigade to a point from which it can prepare the crossing for the 2nd brigade. The six Naval guns now encamped with No. 2 Divisional troops will accompany and act with this brigade division.

9. (Details concerning the positioning of field hospitals, ammunition columns, baggage, supply columns and the pontoon section.)

10. The position of the General Officer Commanding will be near the 4.7-in. guns.

11. Each infantry soldier will carry 150 rounds on his person, the ammunition now carried in the ox wagons of the regimental transport being distributed. Infantry greatcoats will be carried in two ox wagons of regimental transport, if the Brigadiers so wish; other stores will not be placed in these wagons.

12. The General Officer Commanding 6th brigade will detail a half-battalion as Baggage Guard. The two Naval guns now in position immediately south of Divisional Headquarter camp will move at 5 a.m., to the position now occupied by the 4.7-in. guns.

(Although these orders went out in the name of Clery they were effectively Buller's orders.)

The sites today

The Willow Grange battlefield has a few British graves in their original locations. Next to the railway line, where the armoured train was ambushed, is a small mass grave.

On the Colenso battlefield most of Hart's men were buried near where they fell, but their remains were collected and interred in a single mass grave situated at the entrance to the loop. The cemetery is known as Ambleside. The places where the guns of the 14th and 66th batteries stood have been clearly marked. Several British graves and memorials have been relocated from the Colenso town area to the Clouston Garden of Remembrance. This cemetery has some original graves. In addition, the remains of many soldiers from the Thukela Heights have been relocated to here from their original burial sites. A few miles south in the Chieveley cemetery is the grave of Lieutenant FHS Roberts VC.

The Boer trenches around the loop area have almost been obliterated by flooding and agricultural activities. A few low stone walls built by the Boers survive on some low knolls next to the Thukela. Other, southward facing stone walls built by the Boers, survive on the Colenso Koppies. In Colenso there is a small museum with displays on the Anglo-Boer War in the old toll house (next to the original road bridge over the Thukela).

Additional Reading

Amery, L.S. *The Times History of the War in South Africa* Vol II (London, Sampson Low, Marston and Company, 1905).

Barnard, C.J. *Generaal Louis Botha op die Natalse Front, 1899 - 1900* (Cape Town, AA Balkema, 1970).

Breytenbach, J.H. *Die Geskiedenis van die Tweede Vryheidsoorlog in Suid Afrika* Vol II (Pretoria, Die Staatsdrukker, 1969-1978).

Pakenham, Thomas. *The Boer War* (Johannesburg, Jonathan Ball, 1979).

Symons, J. *Buller's Campaign* (London, The Cresset Press, 1963).

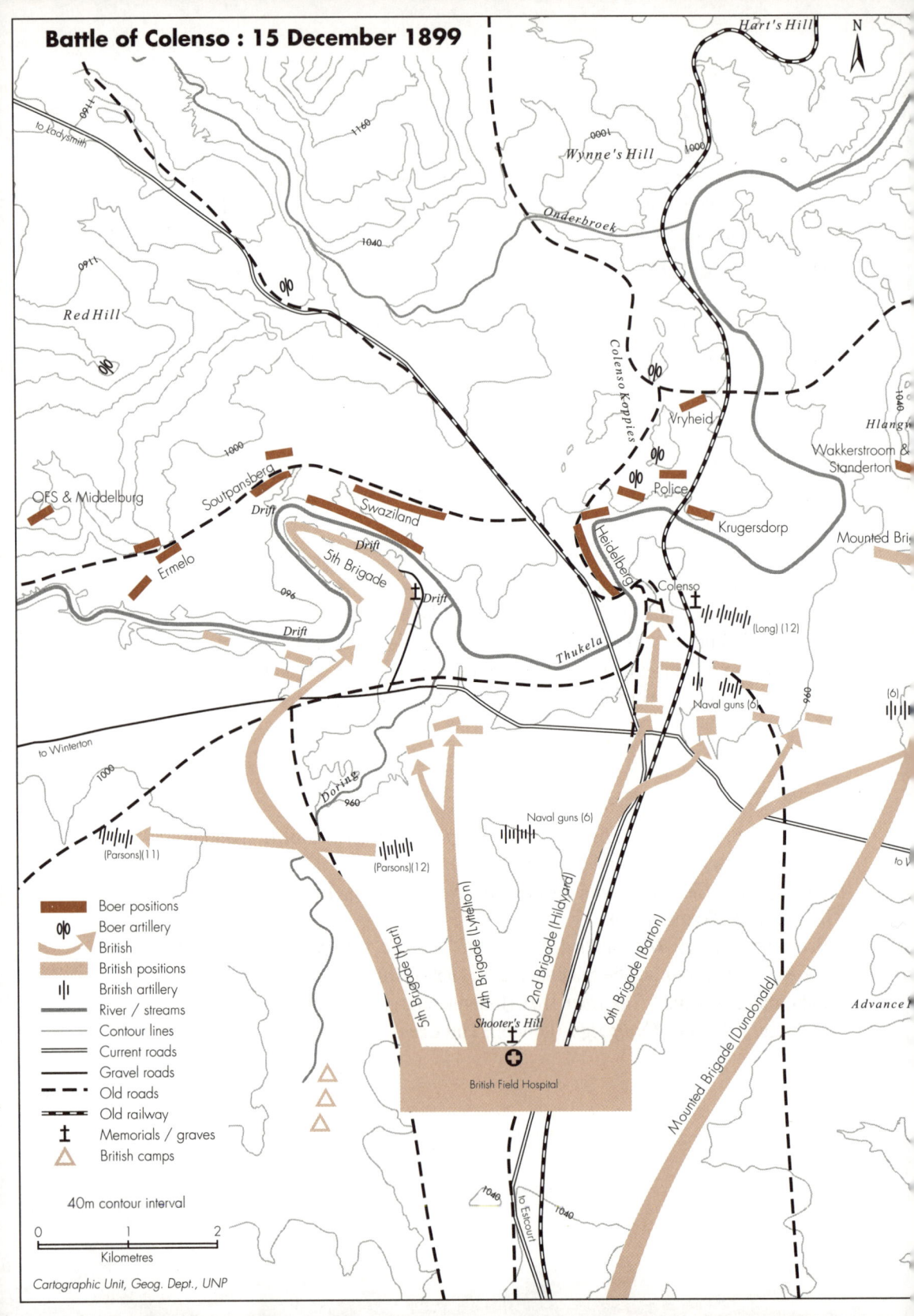

Battle of Colenso : 15 December 1899

N

to Ladysmith

1160

1140

Hart's Hill

Wynne's Hill

0001

1000

Onderbroek

1160

1040

Red Hill

1140

1040

Colenso koppies

Vryheid

Hlangi

Wakkerstroom &
Standerton

OFS & Middelburg

1000

Soutpansberg

Drift

Swaziland

Drift

5th Brigade

096

Drift

Drift

Police

Heidelberg

Krugersdorp

Mounted Bri

Ermelo

Drift

Thukela

Colenso

(Long) (12)

096

(6)

to Winterton

1000

Doring

960

Naval guns (6)

Naval guns (6)

to V

(Parsons)(11)

(Parsons) (12)

5th Brigade (Hart)

4th Brigade (Lyttelton)

2nd Brigade (Hildyard)

6th Brigade (Barton)

Mounted Brigade (Dundonald)

Advance I

Shooter's Hill

British Field Hospital

	Boer positions
	Boer artillery
	British
	British positions
	British artillery
	River / streams
	Contour lines
	Current roads
	Gravel roads
	Old roads
	Old railway
	Memorials / graves
	British camps

40m contour interval

0   1   2
Kilometres

to Estcourt

1040

1040

Cartographic Unit, Geog. Dept., UNP

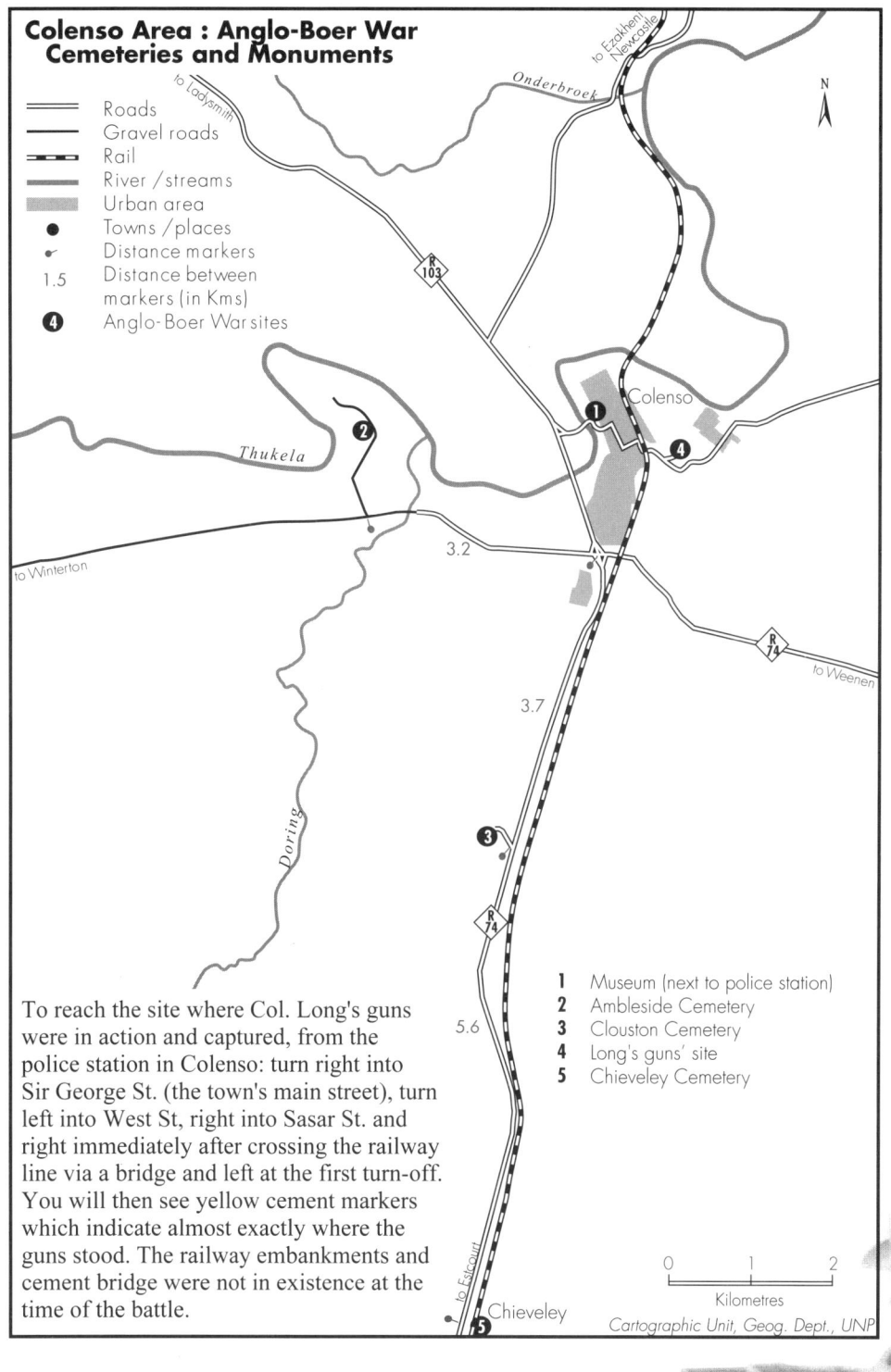

Colenso Area : Anglo-Boer War Cemeteries and Monuments

Roads
Gravel roads
Rail
River/streams
Urban area
Towns/places
Distance markers
1.5 **Distance between markers (in Kms)**
❹ **Anglo-Boer War sites**

to Ezakheni Newcastle

Onderbroek

to Ladysmith

R 103

N

Colenso

❶

❹

Thukela

❷

to Winterton

3.2

R 74

to Weenen

3.7

Doring

❸

R 74

5.6

to Estcourt

Chieveley

❺

1 Museum (next to police station)
2 Ambleside Cemetery
3 Clouston Cemetery
4 Long's guns' site
5 Chieveley Cemetery

To reach the site where Col. Long's guns were in action and captured, from the police station in Colenso: turn right into Sir George St. (the town's main street), turn left into West St, right into Sasar St. and right immediately after crossing the railway line via a bridge and left at the first turn-off. You will then see yellow cement markers which indicate almost exactly where the guns stood. The railway embankments and cement bridge were not in existence at the time of the battle.

0   1   2
Kilometres

Cartographic Unit, Geog. Dept., UNP

⑤